YOUR BRAIN IS YOUR
BIGGEST ENEMY

Mobbesshera Sagir Rayeen

Copyrights

© Mobbesshera Sagir Rayeen 2025

ISBN Number: 9788171922437

All rights reserved. No part of this publication may be reproduced, transmitted, or stored in a retrieval system in any form or by any means without the written permission of the author.

PREFACE

What if I were to tell you that the greatest challenge in your life isn't your situation, your history, or even others—but your own mind? That the thoughts racing through your head, the doubts rising up on you at night, the fears paralyzing you in your tracks—aren't real, but illusions? That the very thing that's meant to lead you is, in fact, your worst enemy?

Sounds melodramatic, I know. But it's not.

Our brains are big, complicated machines—capable of accomplishing astounding things in learning, adaptation, and problem-solving. But this is the twist: they were not created for happiness, success, or fulfillment. They were created for survival. And survival can be a function of clutching fear, being cautious, staying fixed in the known—even if the known is keeping you fixed.

This is not another motivational self-help book with empty encouragement. It is a dive into the war raging in your mind—the battle between the part of you that wants and the part of you that is afraid. It's an exploration of the illusions your brain creates for you—from self-doubt to overthinking, from comparison to fear, from toxic stories to unconscious beliefs that hold you back.

Through over a decade's worth of chapters, we'll reveal to you how your brain is fooling you, why you're stuck in poor habits, and most significantly—how to escape. You'll discover the strength of neuroplasticity, the strategies for rewiring your mind, and the devices to reprogram your thinking from your worst adversary to your greatest ally.

It's not solely science, however. It's about you.

It's about the times you've questioned yourself, the dreams you've given up on, the times you've stared in the mirror, asking yourself if you were good enough. It's about reclaiming control of your mind so that you can finally step into the life you were destined for.

This book will challenge you. It will challenge the stories you have been telling yourself. And if you allow it, it might just revolutionize the way you see yourself for good.

Would you like to break free of the illusions in your mind? Would you like to reboot the thinking that has held you back? Would you like to awaken the champion within you?

INDEX

1	The Silent Saboteur	1
2	The Fear Factory	6
3	The Illusion of Control: How Your Mind Creates A Fake Sense of Power	13
4	Real Risk is Not Uncertainty But Stagnation	21
5	The Myth of Happiness – How Your Brain Sells You a Dream That Doesn't Exist	28
6	The Dopamine Dilemma	34
7	The Inner Critic	43
8	The Stories We Tell Ourselves	50
9	The Comparison Rat Race	61
10	The Power of Reprogramming	71

CHAPTER 1
The Silent Saboteur

Have you found yourself questioning the title of the book? That's other times just another illustration of how you might be misled. It's like a toxic relationship where you start doubting your partner's poisonous behavior and are led into thinking that it's you who is to blame. This book walks you through stories of people who have constantly introspected, believing the fault lies within them, when, in reality, their own minds have been the only thing blocking them from achieving greater advantages.

The Mind as an Obstacle

Have you ever paused just before making that big move? Why are you talking yourself out of taking the chance? Why, although you want to make a move, do you find yourself still in the same patterns? It's not laziness, worthlessness, or incompetence—it's your mind working against you. The very organ that dictates every thought, choice, and action; may also become a problem in the race of your biggest enemy. It can plant seeds of doubt and foster fear while persuading you to settle into your comfort zone. It's like an overwrought parent, too scared to let you into the world. They ignore your goals, desires, and potential in favor of keeping you safe. Sadly, that instinct will often leave you stranded.

When you come up with a brilliant idea, how often does your mind begin bombarding you with reasons that it's not going to work?

"What if you fail?"

"People will just criticize you."

"You're not good enough."

"Maybe later, when you'll be more ready."

Does this ring true to you? That's the quiet saboteur working. It will make you think that playing it safe is the right choice and that taking no risks at all is the most practical option. The thing is, your brain is stuck in survival mode. It is evolved enough to keep you alive.

The Science Behind Self Doubt

Neuroscientists have recently informally defined the human brain as being wired for negativity. The Review of General Psychology explains that our brains give more importance to negative experiences than to positive experiences because they feel wired to do so. Initially, this very system gave an advantage to survive, because actually, the ancestors must memorize the dangers more than the good experience to survive. This tendency often makes room for overthinking, self-doubt, and heightened fear of failure that plagues many people today.

Negativity in self-talk is one of the greatest destructive mental patterns that our mind is bound to indulge in. Studies have shown that inner dialogue produces emotions and self-confidence, in enemy territory, it influences one's physical health. An affirmation such as "I am not good enough" builds inside a belief that sticks later. This is why people unknowingly become trapped in a never-ending cycle of self-doubt and stagnation. The perpetrators are the voices in your head—the critics, the skeptics, the reminders of past failures—which, contrary to reasonable rhetoric, resemble a vicious pattern molded by mere past experiences, societal expectations, and worst of all, unresolved fears.

Cognitive Biases: The Invisible Chains

Feeling-resilient cognitive biases feed the very fire. So, the brain follows some kind of shortcut to get the answer for information faster. But as with all such shortcuts, these always distort reality. You find something called the confirmation bias that shows one has become selective in cognition, processing only that information that supports those fears while willfully ignoring unsubstantiated evidence that says otherwise. If you ever think: that is not going to get done, your mind is going to make sure it ambushes you in the form of a blame game, ballooning every failure, mistake, or negative comment that comes your way into your proof. Then, of course, the spotlight effect assumes that everyone is staring at everything you do, when in truth, most people are too engaged in the busy hustle and bustle of their own lives to notice you at all. The very same biases create that warped sense of reality where failures become inevitable, and the risks seem impossible.

Survival Mode Brain Trap

You're essentially some kind of fricasseed brain hub. It doesn't particularly care whether you are happy, victorious, fulfilled, or an ecstatic cliff diver. Survival for the brain has only one meaning. In the modern world, however, this survival instinct often does more harm than good. The brain could care less whether you are moving ahead in life or not; all it cares for is that you continue to survive. That's why it is keeping you back.

The scenario plays out thus: you want to build a business and change careers or take risks, but no, hold your horses! Do you hesitate? Is it sheer procrastination? No! This is the instinct to survive in you. It sees uncertainty as a life threat; for primitive men, what approached them was an unknown land. Such land was either inhabited by man—eating predators, or they were thrown out of their tribe, which naturally meant certain death. In modern times, the threat could either be blamed on public failure, rejection, or just plain discomfort; but your brain doesn't distinguish between any of these threats. It reacts similarly.

Fear, doubt, and hesitation deaths are bound to fly high every time you feel the need to grow. Your brain is more positive than a head of cyclone eyes. That can entail frantically holding onto a life that feels somehow deadly dull and pointless. According to psychologists, negativity bias is the innate tendency of human behavior to respond more to potential threats than to the rewards that it can offer. Research on this subject seems to show that negative experiences stimulate the amygdala many times more than positive experiences. One rude comment then will send all those hundred compliments dusting. Your mind holds on to its past mistakes as proof that you must not do anything risky whatsoever shortly.

Right here lies the paradox. The same instincts that saved us for centuries are slower than many dreamers to move toward improvement. Comfort zones—once needed for survival—have been, are, and remain invisible cages. That meant people lost risk, sticking to what they knew for fear of peril. Expressing your views during meetings, sharing that art project, or challenging yourself need not carry functional threats. Ignore that because the brain can't tell one threat from another; along the way, it is still scared.

Modern life calls for a new attitude. If you live your life by instinct to survive, you'll always relegate yourself to the default of comfort, which may not be best for your well-being. Growth, success, and fulfillment live on the other side of discomfort. The key is not to eliminate fear but to recognize it for what it is—old programming that no longer serves you.

Breaking Free from the Saboteur

Neuroscience has shown that the brain can be rewired. Through continuous and repeated acts/programming, alongside introducing some exposure and mindset shifts, one can train the mind to see uncertainty as an opportunity instead of danger. This is how people break free from limiting beliefs, build confidence, and step into what was once impossible.

Now that is a thinking process that I'll call it the past. Are you going to go on listening to the older self, the one that keeps you in the very back? Or are you ready to override this old self, the one that has kept you in perpetual survival mode so you can kick-start yourself into the reality you want now?

CHAPTER 2
The Fear Factory

Ever had a racing heart before giving a speech at a meeting? Or, convinced that defeat was sure, pause before that bold move? That is fear working against you, keeping you from living the life you want by speculating about the worst-case scenarios.

It is an instinct to fear because it is something that gives protection. In the modern world, though, it so often turns out to be anxiety, self-doubt, and the constant fear of being criticized. These intangible weights may weigh you back much more than any physical load you may even imagine.

Consider this: Thousands of years ago, you were strolling through a dark forest when all of a sudden, you heard the leaves rustling behind you. Your muscles stiffen, your breath quickens, and your pulse beats faster. You simply react without even thinking. Your brain is your rescuer in such a situation, not your enemy. Turning on the antiquated alarm system meant to defend you from dangers like skulking predators or concealed hazards, is attempting to keep you alive.

Now let's jump forward to today. Your boss emails you with the heading "Meeting at 3 PM," and you sit there in your office staring at it. Your muscles tighten, your breathing accelerates, and your heart starts racing in your chest as that same old alert system is triggered again. The problem is that nothing is out there to get you or any other risk on the horizon. But your head works as if it were.

This is dreadful in action, an evolutionary survival instinct that, although necessary at one point, can now hinder us in ways that our predecessors never experienced.

The Science of Fear: Why You Feel What You Feel

The amygdala is a little, almond-shaped region in your brain that regulates fear. It starts a chain reaction when it perceives or feels a threat. Stress chemicals such as cortisol and adrenaline enter your body, enhancing your attention, raising your heart rate, and priming you for fight-or-flight. Although this reaction was excellent for evading saber-toothed tigers, it is now elicited by public speaking, job interviews, and even sending a dangerous SMS.

Our brains have trouble telling the difference between imagined and genuine threats, according to neuroscientists. Because of this, you may be as afraid to take a professional jump as our ancestors were when confronted with a hungry predator. Happiness is not the brain's fundamental role; survival is. It is concerned with your survival. In actuality, worry is frequently a false alarm. It seeks to keep you safe, yet in doing so it often stops you from fully living.

Fear is an instinctive reaction meant to keep us safe. However, in today's world, it frequently manifests as anxiety, self-doubt, and the ongoing fear of criticism. You may be held back in ways you are unaware of by these unseen weights, which can be more significant than any physical load.

1. The Weight of an Invisible Burden–Anxiety

An anxious person perceives danger in everything, much like an overly watchful father. It is the never-ending "what if?" circle. "What if I make a mistake?" "What if I look foolish?" "What in the world could go wrong?"

The Impact of Anxiety on Emotions

Anxiety is a psychological battleground that goes beyond simple uneasiness. Your mind never truly rested, so you wake up already fatigued. It involves both dreading an unimagined future and repeating previous errors as though you might change history.

Your best moments are snuck into by anxiety, which whispers that they won't last. It convinces you that you're not good enough, causing you to doubt yourself, overthink your remarks, and pause before possibilities. It deprives you of the freedom to simply be—to live without fear hovering over you all the time.

How Anxiety Wreaks Havoc in Life

Imagine being imprisoned behind a glass enclosure. Anxiety keeps you confined, even when you can see the world outside—friends smiling, couples holding hands, people pursuing their ambitions. You want to connect, interact, and live. However, that glass wall feels indestructible because of the dread of shame, failure, or condemnation.

Anxiety sows the seeds of uncertainty in relationships. "Are they genuinely fond of me?" "What if I make a dumb comment?" It turns love into a battleground of uncertainty by making connection feel dangerous. Anxiety in the workplace causes choices to feel like life-or-death choices. Because the agony of stasis is less terrible than the dread of change, people continue to work at unfulfilling employment.

2. Fear of Failure: The Illusion of Perfection

You were most likely taught at some time in your life that errors are a sign of inadequacy and that failure is terrible. But what's the truth? Failure is the cornerstone of all success stories.

How Your Fear of Failing Keeps You Mediocrity

The hidden power that persuades you to settle is your fear of failing. It conveys the message that taking chances isn't worthwhile and that failing at something is worse than never attempting at all. It is the cause of people giving up on their hobbies, remaining in unhealthy relationships, or not pursuing their goals. Do you believe that all of the great artists, inventors, and businesspeople got it right the first time? No. But instead of being a necessary step toward success, fear makes individuals believe that failure is evidence of weakness.

A Life Filled with "What Ifs"

Imagine an elderly guy sitting by himself, thinking back on his life. He has no regrets about the things he tried and didn't succeed at. He feels remorse for the things he never dared to do. A life full of "what ifs" rather than memories results from a fear of failing.

And in actuality, perfection is a myth. Nobody survives life without making mistakes or experiencing failures. The true tragedy is never taking the first step at all, not falling.

3. The Burden of Existing for Others

Because humans are social beings, we are inherently concerned with the opinions of others. However, this terror can occasionally turn incapacitating.

How many decisions did you make in your life to win over someone else? How many times have you suppressed your actual wishes out of fear of rejection, ridicule, or misunderstanding?

Being afraid of being judged is like being in a never-ending trial where every decision, every word, and every action is closely examined. What's the worst? The jury is a creation of our imaginations and isn't real.

Cost of seeking approvals

Living for approval wears you out. People are forced into relationships they don't want, occupations they don't enjoy, and lives that don't fit them. It prevents people from being authentic, from standing out, and from speaking their truth.

The most depressing thing? Most of the time, the individuals we work so hard to win over are too preoccupied with their anxieties to notice our shortcomings. Nevertheless, we let our entire lives be dictated by our dread of their opinions.

The Dark Side: How Addiction Is Caused by These Fears

Self-destruction is among the most terrible outcomes of worry, fear of failing, and dread of being judged. People go for relief—often in the wrong places when their terror becomes intolerable.

Drugs and alcohol provide a short-term diversion from the constant strain. Sometimes, addiction is about numbing suffering rather than about pursuing pleasure. People use alcohol to numb their nervousness. To feel as though their shortcomings are unimportant, they turn to narcotics. To avoid dealing with the life they feel stuck in, they withdraw into diversions.

However, the respite is seldom long-lasting. They are caught in an even more sinister loop as the high wears off and terror returns with more vigor.

Fear Is a Liar—But You Can Outsmart It

You cannot get rid of fear since it is ingrained in your brain. You can, however, teach yourself to react differently. Here's how:

1. The next time you feel afraid, ask yourself, "Is this a real threat, or is this just my brain overreacting?" The latter is the case most of the time.
2. Reframe the Story: Consider fear a green light rather than a stop sign. When you are going to perform something significant, fear appears. Try expressing "I'm excited" rather than "I'm scared."
3. Take Small Risks: Fear becomes weaker the more you fight it. Begin by taking little, doable risks—

speak up at a meeting, try something new, and challenge yourself daily to step a little beyond your comfort zone.
4. Use Your Fear as a Guide: If something makes you feel afraid, it's worthwhile. Fear is frequently a sign of development. Do as you are told.
5. Override the Response: By calming the amygdala, deep breathing, meditation, and mindfulness exercises can lessen the intensity of fear.

Although fear is an age-old weapon, it frequently works against us in the modern world. In an attempt to defend yourself, your brain may end up becoming your biggest barrier. The good news is that you can override its antiquated programming.

Put fear in the passenger seat rather than allowing it to take control. Respect it and acknowledge it, but don't allow it to control your decisions. The life you desire lies just beyond fear. All you need to do is take a step forward.

At that point, you start living your life.

CHAPTER 3
Illusion of Control: How Your Mind Creates a False Sense of Power

We walk through life, thinking we're in control of everything—our future, our relationships, our success. We believe that if we plan enough, prepare enough, or worry enough, we can prevent failure, avoid pain, and make everything come out just as we expect. Reality has other plans. Life is unpredictable, and no amount of planning can safeguard us from setbacks, disappointments, or twists and turns that will surely pop up. However, our brains assure us that things are under control, setting up this false security which leads to greater stress and frustration when things go off track. This illusion is the result of the driving force in our brains to identify patterns, predict the future, and create a sense of order in a far-from-ordered world.

Overthinking: The Mental Hamster Wheel

Because of the way our brain is built to look for solutions, it may fool us into thinking that overanalyzing a situation would somehow provide us clarity and control. Overthinking leads us to feel that we can predict every conceivable conclusion and choose the best course of action if we examine a problem for a sufficient amount of time.

We persuade ourselves that thinking too much equates to preparedness and that reliving previous errors will help us avoid regrets in the future. However, overanalyzing is a mental prison that prevents us from taking action and leaves us paralyzed and nervous. Our level of uncertainty increases as we do more analysis. Overanalyzing exacerbates our fears and makes issues seem more significant than they are, rather than bringing us insight.

Our level of uncertainty increases as we do more analysis. Overanalyzing exacerbates our fears and makes issues seem more significant than they are, rather than bringing us insight. It pulls us out of the present moment, paralyzes action, and intensifies uncertainty and anxiety. We become caught up in a never-ending cycle of insecurity, overthinking, and hesitancy that eventually keeps us from experiencing life to the fullest. We become psychologically weary from this never-ending loop and lose the ability to enjoy the here and now.

Perfectionism: The Mirage of Safety

It makes our brain feel that perfection means safety. Without flaws, if everything is performed flawlessly, then there won't be a critique, denial, or defeat. This elementary requirement is also obtained from the fact that the brain instinctively saves us from social exclusion and disappointment. Right from childhood, we have learned that perfection means achievement. Success and freedom from criticism will undoubtedly follow flawless performance. But perfection is an unattainable ideal that only leads to stress, burnout, and dissatisfaction. It convinces us that if something isn't perfect, it's not worth doing at all. This fear of imperfection results in procrastination, avoiding risks, and holding back from opportunities.

Rather than being essential milestones toward development, mistakes turn into personal failures. We equate our value with our accomplishments, thinking that we are unworthy if we fall short of unrealistic expectations. We lose growth, creativity, and mental tranquility when we strive for perfection. No matter how much we achieve, the pressure to always be perfect wears us out and leaves us feeling like we are falling short. We should strive for development rather than perfection, as perfection is an unachievable goal.

The Certainty Trap: Why We Fear the Unknown

Uncertainty makes the human brain uncomfortable. As it identifies the unknown with possible danger, it craves predictability. For this reason, we often make rigid plans, worry about the worst-case scenario, and have a hard time adjusting. We demand to know that our choices will please us, that the ones we love won't hurt us, and that the things we've planned will occur exactly as we envision. Life doesn't work that way. We experience pain in proportion to how much we seek reassurance. It locks us into a fantasy that we can have control, keeps us from being able to risk ourselves, and engenders persistent anxiety.

The more we strive for assurance, the more we suffer. It traps us in the delusion that we have control, inhibits us from taking chances, and causes ongoing worry. For no other reason than the dread of the unknown, many individuals continue to live in unfulfilling circumstances. Our quest for complete certainty causes us to overthink, over-plan, and worry while also depriving us of the capacity to appreciate life as it comes. In actuality, uncertainty is the very nature of existence and not its enemy. Accepting it can help us find genuine freedom and free ourselves from needless misery.

But the effects of our brain's dishonesty may go well beyond the daily battles of overanalyzing, perfectionism, and anxiety. Some people develop serious mental health issues that make life even more difficult as a result of this delusion of control. The brain's desperate attempts to bring order out of chaos are at the heart of disorders like obsessive-compulsive disorder (OCD) and attention-deficit/ hyperactivity disorder (ADHD). The mind may spiral into cycles of compulsions, hyperactivity, and upsetting ideas that interfere with day-to-day functioning when it is overpowered by its tricks.

> **Control Becomes a Prison in Obsessive-Compulsive Disorder (OCD)**

One of the best illustrations of how the brain's delusion of control may develop into a crippling disorder is OCD. Extreme anxiety brought on by intrusive, upsetting thoughts drives people with OCD to resort to obsessive actions in an attempt to recover control. The brain deceitfully tells individuals that following strict routines, checking locks often, or washing their hands excessively will stop the tragedy. However, this becomes a never-ending trap. The more compulsions are used to manage fears, the stronger those fears become. OCD patients are unable to escape the false demands of their minds and instead find themselves trapped in a relentless cycle of obsession and compulsion. This disorder is a cruel brain trick that takes away a person's capacity to feel safe in their thoughts. It has nothing to do with being extremely tidy or careful.

➢ Defeating a Restless Mind with Attention-Deficit/Hyperactivity Disorder (ADHD)

Another example of how the brain's misguided attempts at control may cause chaos is ADHD. Although ADHD is sometimes misinterpreted as only a lack of attention, it is essentially a conflict between impulsivity and structure. The ADHD brain struggles to focus attention, which makes it difficult to keep control over thoughts, behaviors, and obligations. It needs novelty and excitement. Chronic restlessness, forgetfulness, and trouble finishing duties result from this, which irritates relationships, the workplace, and educational institutions. The person with ADHD may have a strong desire to maintain productivity and organization, but their brain is always pulling them in multiple directions.

Ironically, to control this chaos, the brain frequently produces hyperfixation—intense, all-consuming attention on one thing while ignoring everything else. People with ADHD feel as though they are always failing to keep control over their minds because of this contradiction, which makes it extremely difficult to balance priorities.

Embracing Uncertainty: Training the Mind for a Balanced Life

Because our brain yearns for consistency, it fears unpredictability. It teaches us that we are susceptible if we don't know everything and don't foresee every scenario. In actuality, however, life is inherently unpredictable. We get more nervous and agitated the more we fight it. We must teach our brains to accept the concept that not everything must be under our control and to coexist with uncertainty rather than resist it. The path to acceptance is learning to adjust and move with life, not about giving up.

Mindfulness training is one of the most effective strategies for preparing the brain for uncertainty. By practicing mindfulness, we may learn to stop worrying about the uncertain future and instead concentrate on the here and now. We may lessen the mental fatigue caused by overthinking and start to understand that we don't have to manage everything by focusing on the now. A calmer, more tranquil life is possible when we practice mindfulness, which also helps us separate from the delusion of certainty. Another important step is to change how we think about failure. Because they view any mistake as catastrophic, many people suffer from perfectionism. Failure, however, is not a goal; rather, it is only a component of the growth process. The more we fear failure, the more we avoid challenges and are trapped in a constructive attitude. By interpreting failure as an opportunity to progress rather than a personal weakness, we free ourselves from the exhausting weight of continuously trying to be in control.

There has also to be developed resilience, a capacity for bouncing back. While not impervious to misfortune, one is capable of overcoming it. Life is sure to offer unpredictable obstacles at times, but the secret lies in developing that inner strength that enables one to face and defeat them, instead of backing away. It is about understanding that we have done it before—embracing pain, and living with ambiguity.

Resilience teaches us that we are not powerless, even when the brain tells us otherwise. Learning to let go is equally vital. Knowing what we can and cannot control is the key to the skill of letting go, which is not the same as disregarding issues or obligations. We use a great deal of mental energy attempting to correct problems that are just beyond our control. We make room for calm, creativity, and mental health when we deliberately let go of the desire to manage every part of our lives.

Finally, it's important to put self-compassion first. Our brain may be our most harshest critic, always telling us that we are not doing enough or that we are failing at life. But in reality, no one knows everything. One of the best ways to lessen mental stress is to be kind to ourselves when we deal with uncertainty. We can go forward with clarity and confidence when we have self-compassion, which allows us to accept our challenges without letting them define who we are.

By educating our minds to embrace uncertainty instead of fearing it, we provide ourselves the chance to live a lighter, more free, and incalculably more fulfilling life. The brain constantly tries to convince us that control is the answer, yet real peace is letting go.

Our Brain Deceives Us

Our minds have a habit of creating illusions. It gives the impression that by micromanaging every eventuality, getting fussy about every detail, and predicting everything's aftermath we can impact results. Yet the illusion of control is essentially an adaptation, once useful, no longer of our modern circumstances. The point of fact remains, that nothing's going to become predictable once it is alive. Exhaustion, disappointment, and frustration are the only results of clinging to control. We need to see this lie and change the way we think. We should prioritize self-trust, resilience, and adaptation above trying to control everything. We can eventually escape control and live more comfortably once we realize that it is a myth.

It's not that we can't do anything about things; it's the way we react to those things. The opposite of surrender is not opposition but adjustment to change, not relinquishment. Failure and error are a fact of life, but they define neither our worth nor our success. No rigid planning would ever have accommodated the possible joys, progress, and possibilities inherent in embracing the uncertainty of life.

The objective of life is to learn how to handle uncertainty with confidence, not control everything. The freedom from the illusion of control brings greater calmness, less tension, and more space for spontaneity in daily life. We must trust and believe in our ability to navigate anything life brings us.

CHAPTER 4
Real risk is not uncertainty but stagnation

Comfort zones have the sense of a cozy, well-known hug. They offer convenience, regularity, and security. Desiring stability is perfectly okay; the issue arises when comfort becomes a source of stagnation. The ever-protective brain tells us that the best course of action is to stay inside known bounds. Comfort zones, however, may be misleading; what appears to be security is sometimes actually a constraint. We stop learning, we stop developing, and most importantly, we stop experiencing life to the fullest.

➢ **The Slow Poison of Stagnation**

Motion is life. Instead of being a single achievement, growth is an ongoing process. The moment we stop challenging ourselves, we begin to decline. Stasis gradually takes shape over time, disguised as regularity, risk aversion, or the rationalization that "things are fine as they are." Our potential is progressively diminished by this way of thinking. Because the alternative change seems so overwhelming, we remain where we are despite feeling uninspired, restless, and confined.

Imagine a pond that isn't moving. The water becomes cloudy, stops flowing, and finally turns to mush, which attracts insects and algae. Our minds function quite similarly. The drive wanes, the abilities weaken, and the concepts get stale in the absence of challenges and change. The slowest kind of self-sabotage is staying still, even when it feels safe.

➤ Fear: The Gatekeeper of Comfort Zones

Why do we remain confined to our comfort zones? Fear. Fear of judgment, fear of failure, and dread of uncertainty. The mind magnifies all the worst-case possibilities and persuades us that leaving our comfort zone is dangerous. But the reality is that suffering and progress go hand in hand. Nobody ever becomes great without experiencing some degree of suffering. Every successful individual, inventor, and game-changer has had to overcome their fear and take a risk. We unwittingly give up our potential to a life of mediocrity when we allow fear to control our decisions.

➤ The Power of Discomfort: How to Break Free

Discomfort is a sign of progress, not the enemy. Parts of your brain that thrive on adaptability are activated when you push yourself, whether that be by taking on new tasks, establishing a new career, or placing yourself in novel circumstances. Your resilience increases, your confidence rises, and all of a sudden, what was once frightening becomes instinctive.

Making tiny, deliberate changes is a terrific approach to reprogramming your brain to welcome suffering. Start by speaking in small groups if public speaking makes you nervous. Try new cuisine or an alternative route home if you're feeling more daring. The secret is to convince your brain that discomfort is an opportunity rather than a sign of danger.

➢ Toxic Comfort: When Safe Spaces Become Cages

Sometimes we remain in circumstances because they are comfortable for us rather than because they are healthy. For instance, relationships can turn into a comfort zone. We stay even when affection turns into dominance, concern into manipulation, and warmth becomes icy quiet. The brain deceives us into thinking that this is the best we can do, that it would be too dangerous to leave, and that we are the issue rather than the poisonous situation we are in. We blame ourselves, make excuses, and believe that things will improve if we only put forth more effort. However, some comfort zones are just gilded prisons that keep us mired in self-doubt and constricting ideas.

➢ The Loneliness Dilemma: Settling for the Wrong People

Another sneaky element that traps us is loneliness. We may enter connections and relationships that don't reflect who we are because we are afraid of being alone. We find ourselves surrounded by individuals whose energy drains us and whose beliefs don't align with our own, but we persuade ourselves that being with them is preferable to being alone. Is it, though? The presence of those who make you feel alone is what constitutes true loneliness, not the absence of others. We give up our mental well-being for fleeting solace when we cling to the wrong company, only to end ourselves more adrift than before.

➢ Bed Rotting: The Silent Spiral into Apathy

One of the most frequent outcomes of being stuck in one's comfort zone is "bed rotting." A person who spends inordinate amounts of time in bed, scrolling aimlessly, consuming limitless amounts of information, or napping only to escape reality is engaging in a deep withdrawal from life, which goes beyond simply taking a day off to relax. It first appears to be a safe, even essential, stress-reduction strategy. However, it eventually turns into a self-imposed exile. In this downward cycle, the brain is an important player. It persuades you that the easiest and safest course of action is to remain in bed. "Why get up when you can escape the world's expectations?" It murmurs. "Why try when failure is a possibility?" The issue is that it gets more difficult to get out of bed, the longer you remain there. Because the brain is made to go for the easiest route, it begins to associate effort with pain and inactivity with comfort. Guilt creeps in, motivation wanes, and what once felt like a haven becomes a prison, and so the cycle goes on.

Because it poses as self-care, this practice is very risky. You pretend that you're simply "resting," but you're avoiding it. Avoiding obligations, suffering, and the opportunity to show oneself incorrect. You grow increasingly estranged from your goals, your relationships, and life itself the longer you engage in this activity. Your brain has effectively persuaded you that hiding is preferable to facing the world, all because of its desire for convenience. In actuality, the issues you are trying to escape will still be there when you wake up, only they will feel even bigger. This is true regardless of how long you spend in bed.

➤ The Death of Passion: When Comfort Kills Creativity and Ambition

The gradual deterioration of academic goals, professional objectives, and personal passions is another pernicious consequence of becoming overly comfortable. It never occurs simultaneously. You miss a day at the gym first. Then you put off doing that artistic endeavor. Your brain tells you, "I'll do it tomorrow." However, tomorrow becomes next week, then next month, and before you know it, you won't even be able to recall the last time you genuinely did anything that ignited your spirit. The brain begins to prioritize short-term comfort above long-term pleasure because it is addicted to rapid gratification and easy dopamine from scrolling, eating junk food, or watching TV. It persuades you that following your aspirations is too demanding, too unpredictable, and too time-consuming. So you let them get away with it.

Once-pleasurable hobbies now feel like labor. Your once-exciting career aspirations now appear unachievable. Your passion for learning, producing, and growing fades and eventually vanishes. What's the worst? You aren't even aware of it until you wake up one day feeling empty, as if something is absent. As if you're not there. Your brain has deprived you of achievement, advancement, and purpose to shield you from failure. Comfort zones destroy dreams in this way: they gradually persuade you to let go of them rather than ripping them away.

It takes an intentional revolt against the trickery of your brain to break away from this pattern. It entails exerting oneself even when you don't want to. It entails realizing that although effort will always seem awkward at first, it is not inherently bad. Bring back the passions you once had. Get back in touch with the goals you set aside. Because one day you'll wake up and realize that if you let your brain keep you confined to comfort, you wasted more than just time.

➤ The True Cost of Staying Comfortable

It is easy to ignore the effects of staying in our comfort zones since they take time to become apparent. But where do you see yourself a few years from now? Are you doing well or are you feeling trapped and wishing you had taken a different course of action? Those who refuse to adapt often experience regret. They lament the life they may have had if they had the guts to step outside of their comfort zone, the chances they lost, and the goals they put off.

Self-assurance, not fear of the unknown, should be the source of true comfort. The true difficulty is in escaping toxic situations, realizing when familiarity is dangerous, and discovering inner calm. Growth entails recognizing when our comfort zones have become constraints, but it does not need flinging ourselves into turmoil all the time. You owe it to yourself to take action and reclaim your potential if a circumstance, relationship, or routine is preventing you from reaching your full potential. Because remaining where you don't belong is the true risk, not venturing into the unknown.

Life is not too careful to be experienced, studied, and tested. If you feel stuck, ask yourself if you're at peace or afraid. Your brain will always select safety, but you have so much more potential than you do now. Learn to accept uncertainty, get over your fear, and explore the countless opportunities waiting for you.

Growth is uncomfortable. It may be chaotic, erratic, and even frightening at times. However, that is also where the magic takes place. The most memorable encounters, the closest bonds, and the most profound epiphanies all take place away from the familiar.

Your brain will attempt to maintain the appearance of safety, but the objective is satisfaction, not safety. Put yourself to the test. Take chances. Venture fearlessly into the unknown. Because when you do, you'll see that the biggest risk was never the actual danger, but rather the regret of never attempting.

CHAPTER 5
The Myth of Happiness–How Your Brain Sells You a Dream That Doesn't Exist

Joy—the final objective, the point at which we are all racing. However, have you ever observed that the sense of contentment you get never lasts, regardless of what you accomplish or the milestone you reach? Suddenly, you're considering a better job after landing your desired one. After finding love, you start to question whether something more thrilling exists. After achieving your objectives, you quickly create new ones. Happiness seems to be an illusion, constantly present but never achievable.

Why this never-ending chase? Your need for more is ingrained in your brain. It persuades you that pleasure is attainable and that all you need to do is put in more effort, make more money, and perform better. Happiness, however, is a dynamic goal that changes every time you approach it, rather than a fixed destination. And the most inhumane part? Your brain does this on purpose.

The Brain's Cruel Trick: Keeping You Dissatisfied on Purpose

Your brain is programmed to think that what you have is insufficient, so it is always looking for what comes next— not because you truly need something better. It functions similarly to an algorithm meant to keep you scrolling, except your life is used in place of social media. Even when you accomplish a goal, your brain immediately normalizes the achievement and creates new desires, making it seem hard to be pleased. Because their minds are constantly looking for the next item, those who appear to "have it all" frequently report feeling empty.

Dopamine, the neurotransmitter in charge of motivation and reward, is used to achieve this. The hitch is that dopamine has nothing to do with pleasure. It's about looking forward to enjoyment. Dopamine is released by your brain when you pursue an objective rather than when you succeed. Because of this, the prospect of achievement seems more thrilling than the actuality of it. Your brain has deceived you into thinking that the next thing will eventually provide you with long-lasting happiness, which is why you desire it rather than because you need it. It never does, to give you a hint.

The "If-Only" Lie: The Happiness Illusion

Your brain can manipulate things very well. It continuously perpetuates the "If-Only" fallacy, which holds that you would be content if you had more money, were in a relationship, or had a particular appearance. Because you constantly think that happiness is just out of grasp, you live your entire life trying to find the next greatest thing. The high, however, is fleeting when you do reach it. The brain immediately adjusts the goalposts and normalizes your achievement. Your new baseline is swiftly established by the item that once appeared to be a dream.

This is known as the "hedonic treadmill", a psychological phenomenon in which you consistently reach your prior level of happiness regardless of what happens. Have you ever won the lotto? You'll be thrilled—for a long time. After that, you'll adapt. Experienced a setback? You'll feel sad at first, but you'll get used to it gradually. Because it wants you to keep going, the brain makes sure that no accomplishment ever results in lasting enjoyment.

The Psychology of Diminishing Returns on Happiness

The results of psychologists' considerable research on happiness are startling. According to studies, even significant life events like marriage, purchasing a dream home, or receiving a promotion don't guarantee happiness in the long run. Rather, our brains adjust to new situations fast. This phenomenon, known as brain adaptation, explains why an accomplishment that once seemed to change your life later becomes simply another typical aspect of your existence.

The False Promises of Material and External Success

An accomplishment first causes an overpowering wave of excitement. But that thrill wears off with time. Consider it like eating your favourite food—it tastes great the first time, but it becomes boring if you eat it every day. The same holds for relationships, financial success, and even individual achievements. Over time, the more we acquire, the less value we find in those items. We have a never-ending need for something novel and more exciting in place of genuine fulfillment. Happiness is a never-ending cycle, but our brains tell us that it will be found in the next great item.

The notion that happiness can be purchased is something that our society continuously promotes. Advertisements promise you happiness if you get the newest technology, a larger home, or a new automobile. You are constantly exposed to pictures of individuals with seemingly ideal lives on social media. However, the reality is that none of these things provide happiness that lasts.

Material riches have been shown to have declining benefits on happiness in positive psychology research. Having more money doesn't make you any happier if your fundamental necessities are satisfied. However, society persuades us that it will, which pushes us to prioritize material achievement above our mental health. The idea that "just a little more" can ultimately make you feel whole is reinforced by the brain, which contributes to this.

Escaping the Illusion: How to Rewire Your Brain for Real Happiness

Therefore, where does happiness originate if it cannot be found in material accomplishments? Training your brain to stop pursuing and start living is the solution. Real happiness is something you practice rather than something you can acquire. It results from being able to enjoy the here and now, from separating oneself from the never-ending cycle of want, and from comprehending that your brain has been deceiving you all along.

You Must Change the Brain's Normal Settings to Escape This Trap

Identify the Pattern: The first stage is awareness. Pause when you hear your mind say, "I'll be happy when..." The delusion is speaking there.

Retrain Your Reward System: Rather than striving for the next big item, begin to find happiness in the little things in life. The sun's warmth, a meaningful discussion, and the sense of advancement rather than merely outcomes.

Disengage from the Destination Mentality: Happiness has no end. Eliminate the idea that life is a race with a finish line. The voyage itself is the source of the delight.

Actively cultivate gratitude—not as a platitude, but as a genuine brain workout. Make your brain concentrate on what is currently there instead of what is missing, as this is how it is wired.

Rethink Success and Fulfillment: Rather than gauging happiness by accomplishments outside of yourself, gauge it by how satisfied, peaceful, and present you feel every day.

Philosophical and Real-Life Perspective

Happiness, according to ancient thinkers like the Stoics, is about wanting what you already have rather than obtaining what you desire. Buddhism and other Eastern philosophies hold that suffering stems from clinging to wants. These concepts have scientific support in addition to being spiritual. You feel more at ease when you have fewer cravings.

Those who have learned to appreciate everything are the ones who have escaped the illusion of happiness, not those who own everything. The happiest people aren't those who have it all, but rather those who have taught their brains to be happy with what they have, whether they be monks living simply or mindfulness practitioners.

Cost of Chasing Happiness

The emotional weariness that results from continuously chasing the next great thing is even more worrisome. Burnout, anxiety, and persistent restlessness are caused by the never-ending cycle of success, comparison, and discontent. Many people wake up one day and discover that they still feel empty on the inside, even when they have everything they believe they want. This is because, instead of developing happiness inside themselves, their brain has trained them to look for it outside of themselves.

Relationships are also impacted by this ongoing discontent. Whether in friendships, employment, or personal relationships, those who are constantly looking for something "better" frequently suffer from commitment. They are unable to truly appreciate and engage in the present because they believe that something better is always out there. This kind of thinking weakens interpersonal relationships over time, making people feel alone and alienated.

The drive to do better at work can result in toxic productivity when individuals base their value on their output. In the pursuit of achievement, they forgo their enjoyment, leisure, and self-care. However, they frequently find themselves feeling exhausted rather than satisfied at the end of the day.

CHAPTER 6
The Dopamine Dilemma

Pleasure is ingrained in our brains. It makes us believe that happiness awaits us in the next surge of fullfilment, seek what feels good, and staying away from what feels awful. The issue is that our brains are addicts. It just seeks immediate enjoyment and is indifferent to long-term contentment. We are now trapped in a never-ending loop of want, reward, and disappointment since the same thing that was supposed to keep us motivated for survival has turned against us.

Here, the enemy is not just the outside world that lures us in with distractions, but also our imaginations. Even while doing things that cause pain, our brain's obsession with happiness compels us to participate in activities that provide us with momentary dopamine boosts. This explains our compulsive social media browsing, binge-watching, overindulging in unhealthy eating, and pursuing fleeting acceptance from others. We are ensnared by the dopamine-driven cycle, which makes self-control appear painful and makes indulgence seem like salvation. However, we jeopardize our health when we give in to the demands of our brain.

The Brain's Need for Instant Gratification

The brain was essentially designed to seek pleasure and avoid suffering. By helping us find food, housing, and other people, this system is utilized to keep us alive. This survival tactic, however, fails in contemporary society where everything is instantly available. Why make an effort to accomplish anything when a shortcut is just a click away? Why endure boredom when there is so much entertainment to choose from? The brain can no longer distinguish between artificial, fleeting rewards and real, meaningful ones; it now only requires dopamine, quick and easy.

This vulnerability has been weaponized by materialism and modern technology. Without any genuine closeness, social media creates the appearance of a social relationship. Our sense of taste is taken over by processed foods, which renders wholesome meals tasteless. Rapid entertainment and short-form material have rewired our attention spans, making in-depth work seem unattainable. We are unaware that each time we indulge in these momentary gratifications, our brains are trained to put pleasure ahead of long-term achievement.

The terrible irony is that our level of satisfaction decreases as we strive for more dopamine. The reason for this is because our brain develops tolerance. What started as an exhilarating rush quickly turned into the new normal, and we started requiring an increased amount of stimulation to experience the same degree of pleasure. This is the reason addiction is so harmful, whether it be drugs, entertainment, or even approval. It begins as an innocent item that gives us a sense of well-being, but it gradually swallows us and leaves us feeling even more lost.

Resilience and patience are also destroyed by this cycle. We lose the potential to strive for significant accomplishments if we constantly treat ourselves to quick gratification. When amusement is so much simpler, why dedicate yourself to acquiring a skill? When there is an easy way out, why put up with discomfort? It gets increasingly difficult to find delight in everyday, basic events the more we fall into this trap.

The Science Behind Habits, Addiction, and Social Media Manipulation

The Habit Loop and How It Forms

Efficiency is highly valued by our brain. It's better if it can automate more. Because of this, both positive and negative behaviours get ingrained in our everyday lives. In his book, The Power of Habit, Charles Duhigg outlines a three-step brain loop—cue, routine, and reward—that controls the creation of habits. Our brain begins to want an activity before we even carry it out when we consistently link it to a reward. This loop strengthens itself over time, making it very challenging to change bad habits.

For example, many people have developed the practice of checking their phones first thing in the morning. The dopamine rush from alerts, texts, and news updates is the reward, the trigger is waking up, and the habit is picking up the phone and scrolling. This behaviour becomes so ingrained in our everyday lives that it becomes very hard to break. The frightening part? These behaviours are designed to keep us interested and wanting more; they are not established by accident.

How Addiction Takes Hold

A common misconception about addiction is that it's only due to a lack of willpower. However, the truth is that the reward system in the brain is disrupted, which is a deeply ingrained neurological problem. Our brain begins developing a tolerance when we expose ourselves to short bursts of dopamine regularly, whether through social media, alcohol, drugs, or junk food. This indicates that the same amount of stimuli no longer results in the same level of enjoyment. We gradually develop reliance and addiction as a result of needing more of the same action to get similar feeling.

When it comes to digital addiction, this issue is very apparent. Social networking sites are made with dopamine-influencing features like autoplay, push notifications, and endless scrolling. Because of the endless cycle of reward and hunger that our electronics produce, we find it very difficult to put them down. The more we participate, the more our brains are rewired to favour these short-lived pleasures over longer-term, more significant benefits like hobbies, in-person relationships, and personal development.

The Role of Social Media Manipulation

We are not as aware of our mental flaws as social media businesses are. Maximizing user engagement, or keeping consumers clicking, browsing, and interacting for as long as possible, is the foundation of their whole business strategy.

They accomplish this by using carefully constructed algorithms to take advantage of our psychological weaknesses. To get users to come back for more, these platforms employ strategies like personalized content, social validation metrics (likes, comments, shares), and sporadic payouts (like slot machines).

The way social media platforms make use of FOMO (fear of missing out) is a prime illustration of this manipulation. We are driven to keep returning, comparing, and interacting when we see other people sharing carefully manicured pictures of their lives. This leads to a vicious cycle in which we become reliant on social media for affirmation in addition to becoming addicted to it. The algorithm continuously adjusts material to keep us interested, and the more we interact with it, the more it creates a never-ending cycle of digital reliance.

How to Regain Control and Build Discipline

To know we are not helpless is where the solution lies. The first step toward escaping the lure of today's technology, driven by dopamine, is to understand how our minds are being tricked. By rewiring our behaviours in more conscious ways, practising mindfulness, and putting boundaries on technology, we could regain control over our lives. If we develop interests in the real world and focus on deep work while putting more emphasis on real human connections and less on technology-mediated ones, our brains could start seeking deep fulfillment rather than instant gratification. We might be able to tilt the balance of nature in our favour by making conscious efforts, even when it is fighting against human nature.

Understanding the Power of Delayed Gratification

Saying no to distractions is only one aspect of the fight against rapid gratification; another involves reprogramming our brains to prioritize long-term development over momentary pleasure. The secret to regaining control in a world that is set up to divert our attention and take advantage of our inclinations is discipline. Discipline, however, is not about self-denial or severe self-punishment. Intentional living, awareness of our brain's inclinations, and utilizing them to our benefit, rather than letting them control us, are all components of true discipline.

Also, one of the main characteristics that distinguishes successful people from strong, surviving ones is the ability to practice delayed gratification. The well-known Stanford Marshmallow Experiment showed that children who resisted the immediate temptation of eating a single marshmallow for a future reward of two fared better later in life. This goes beyond mere willpower and involves training the brain to keep future benefits in sight, rather than surrendering to instant gratification.

Building Self-Discipline Without Burnout

The problem is that our brain, which is based on impulses for immediate survival, opposes this notion. It encourages us to pursue short-term gains rather than long-term gains. This is the reason why spending hours on social media feels natural while sitting down to read a book or practice a skill feels like a job. Our brains need to be trained to seek long-term benefits just as much as they do immediate, uncomplicated pleasures if we want to become disciplined.

The reason most individuals struggle with discipline is because they employ force. They establish strict guidelines, deprive themselves of pleasure, and eventually lose all willpower. Discipline is about strategy, not force, thus this method is bound to fail. Here are some strategies for developing self-discipline that will truly last:

Make It Simple to Begin: Establishing a habit is the most difficult element of all. Start with five minutes of exercise rather than pushing yourself to complete an hour-long session. Read five pages instead of

fifty. Although the brain is resistant to significant change, it swiftly adjusts to modest, doable changes.

Use Temptation Bundling: Mix an enjoyable activity with a task that requires self-control. When working out, only play your favourite podcast. Drink your favourite tea as you write in your journal. If you begin to associate pleasure with output, your brain will begin to associate discipline with joy.

Set Clear Boundaries When Using Technology: Social media and other digital distractions are intended to take your attention away from your work. Set server time limits, employ app blockers, or plan "dopamine detox" days where you don't use any technology at all. This helps to reset the urge for instant pleasure in your brain.

Develop Self-Compassion: An all-or-nothing mentality is the worst destroyer of discipline. You don't fail after one terrible day. Recognize your procrastination or missed workout with a lenient mindset and get back on track instead of condemning yourself. Burnout results from harsh self-criticism, but consistency comes from self-compassion.

Rewiring the Brain for Long-Term Success

We can rewire our habits, actions, and even our attitudes, according to neuroscience. Because of the brain's flexibility, we are not limited by the patterns we exhibit. We may remodel our brain's reward system by regularly selecting delayed gratification, minimizing impulsive actions, and creating a successful environment.

A person's brain will eventually develop to associate pleasure with success rather than external validation if, for instance, they start restricting their usage of social media and instead dedicate time to learning a skill. Although it takes time for this change to occur, self-discipline gradually becomes more of an instinctive response as new brain pathways are formed.

The Long-Term Rewards of Mastering Discipline

Life opens up in unexpected ways when you learn to regulate your urges. Being more present enhances relationships. Because you prioritize in-depth work above distractions, your job thrives. As a result of being freed from the dopamine-driven highs and lows, your mental health stabilizes.

The goal of discipline is freedom, not limitation. The ability to choose what benefits you rather than what makes you feel temporarily numb. The ability to live your life as you see fit, free from outside influences.

The ability to design a future guided by significant objectives and genuine fulfilment rather than ephemeral wants.

Pleasure is what your brain will constantly seek. It is inherently wired that way. However, it is completely up to you to decide what kind of pleasure you want. If you properly train it, it will turn into your best ally rather than your worst adversary.

CHAPTER 7
Inner Critic

The voice in everybody's head says things like, "You don't belong here," "You're not good enough," or "Someone else could do this better." This voice of the inner critic may become one of the greatest enemies to one's success when ignored, breeding uncertainty, fuelling impostor syndrome, and keeping one locked in a deadly loop of fear and procrastination. Ironically, this voice should motivate a person, but it originates from one's mind.

Given the circumstances, technology will invariably become our greatest enemy instead of our greatest ally.

Self-doubt is a deeply rooted survival strategy, not merely a passing emotion. To live, our predecessors needed to maintain social cohesiveness, which meant avoiding rejection, failure, and excessive individuality. Our brain thus becomes hyper-aware of possible dangers, even if they are only hypothetical criticisms or self-imposed expectations. These days, this shows itself as the persistent worry that we are not good enough.

The issue? It is difficult for our brains to distinguish between perceived social risk and actual danger. It has the same panic response when it makes a mistake in a meeting as it would when it comes into contact with a wild animal. We remain in our comfort zones because of this inflated fear of failing, which prevents us from taking chances, pursuing ambitious objectives, or seizing fresh possibilities.

Impostor Syndrome: Feeling Like a Fraud

One of the worst experiences by far that can be visited on the inner critic is impostor syndrome. A chronic belief that our achievement merits little, if any, pride and that, in the longer run, the secret will be out that we're fraudulent. The impostor syndrome makes us feel as if we are fortunate and that any day someone will discover us, whatever our level of aptitude and wisdom.

This phenomenon affects high achievers, creatives, entrepreneurs, and most professionals from various sectors. It is not an issue that is reserved for some. Even some of the most successful people in the world admit that they feel like they do not truly belong. The brain makes us feel incompetent even in the face of overwhelming evidence of our competence.

The truth? Distorted thinking is all that impostor syndrome really is. It feeds on minimizing our accomplishments, comparing ourselves to others, and being ideal. Unchecked, it prevents us from going outside our comfort zones, bargaining for our value, and taking advantage of fresh chances.

Where the Inner Critic Comes from and How to Quiet it

The inner critic is not a coincidence; it is a product of biology, experience, and upbringing. Cultural norms, personal shortcomings, and family dynamics all have an impact on us from a young age. Many of us grow up with subtle or not-so-subtle messages that perpetuate the feeling that we are not enough. Examples of how our brain absorbs and internalizes these messages include comparisons to others, informal remarks from teachers, and high expectations from parents. Eventually, these external evaluations become a recurrent internal monologue that convinces us that we must be perfect to be worthy.

But the inner critic has roots not only in parenting but also in evolution. The existence of our predecessors depended on their ability to accept others. If one was kicked out of a group, death was inevitable. As a result, the human brain becomes extremely sensitive to rejection and is always searching for hints that we could miss. In the current world, this survival tactic often backfires, yet it was helpful when it came to situations where fitting in meant the difference between life and death. Instead of making us safer, it makes us smaller. Because we fear failing, looking dumb, or being rejected, we are hesitant to take chances. An instinct that was once essential for life has now become a self-imposed prison.

We must first acknowledge the inner critic for what it is: a flawed security system that was intended to keep us safe but is now doing more damage than good. Detachment, or distancing oneself from the critical voice, is one effective strategy. "I'm having a thought that I might fail" is a better way to phrase it than "I'm a failure." By putting some space between you and your inner critic, this minor change makes it simpler to question its authority. Another strategy is to substitute self-compassion for self-judgment. Treat yourself like a helpful friend rather than scolding yourself for a mistake. Ask yourself, "Would I talk to someone I love this way?" if you find yourself in a self-doubt spiral. Rewriting the story is necessary if the response is negative.

Another tactic to lessen the inner critic is to actively refute it. The brain is prone to looking for evidence to support its beliefs. If you constantly convince yourself that you are incapable, your brain will reinforce that view by highlighting every mistake. To counter this, record your small triumphs. Write down your successes, courageous moments, or occasions when you overcome doubt. The inner critic may be directly challenged by a number of facts, which would diminish its credibility. The more you challenge yourself, the more evidence you have that you are competent and deserving.

Silence, when it is unquestioned and allowed to control your world, is where the inner critic flourishes. However, its influence diminishes as soon as you begin to challenge its reasoning, reinterpret its messages, and demonstrate its fallacies via action. Since it's a natural part of being human, you don't have to get rid of it entirely, but you can learn to reduce its loudness and stop letting it dictate your decisions. It is completely up to you whether or not you pay attention to this voice, even if it may be present all the time.

Strategies for Building Self-Confidence and Resilience

Resilience and self-assurance are abilities that may be acquired with deliberate effort, practice, and mental changes rather than natural traits. The negative bias refers to the brain's innate tendency to place more weightage on dangers and failures, rather than on accomplishments and strengths.

If we want to develop self-confidence, we must deliberately train our thoughts to look for proof of our skills rather than focus on our flaws.

The Power of Small Wins

Studies in psychology have shown that even small successes boost confidence. Setting and achieving small, manageable goals allows us to show our brain that we can do things; we are competent. These small victories add up over the years to create a foundation of confidence strong enough to withstand life's inevitable blows.

Confidence, then, is the ability to act despite fear—not the absence of fear.

Reframing Failure: The Growth Mindset

The way we view failure is closely related to resilience. People who adopt a growth mindset, as psychologist Carol Dweck advocates, recognize that failure is a learning opportunity rather than a roadblock. We become weak when we view failure as a judgment of our value. In reality, errors ought to be viewed as learning moments.

This reinterpretation of failure enables resilience by converting setbacks into opportunities for development.

The Role of Self-Compassion

Emotionally, self-compassion and self-confidence are related. Many people think that having confidence stems from approval from others, yet genuine confidence stems from how we treat ourselves.

We create an internal support system that fortifies us against outside negativity when we substitute self-kindness for self-criticism.

As Lau Tzu states, "Because one believes in oneself, one does not try to convince others." One doesn't require the approval of others as they are happy with who they are.

Modern Approaches to Tame the Inner Critic

Cognitive behavioural therapy (CBT) and mindfulness: CBT procedures challenge faulty thought patterns, while mindfulness practices assist in monitoring negative self-talk without getting overwhelmed by it.

Journaling: Putting self-doubts in writing and refuting them with reasoning might help lessen their impact.

Digital detox: Reducing social media use can help avoid harmful comparisons and lessen the impact of outside approval.

Visualization and Affirmations: You may remodel brain pathways toward confidence by imagining achievement and repeating positive affirmations.

The Confidence-Exposure Loop

According to neuroscience studies, fear is weakened by exposure and strengthened by avoidance.

We teach our brains to cope with discomfort and adjust each time we face uncertainty.

Fundamentally, confidence is a habit that becomes stronger each time we decide to be brave instead of hesitant, and fearful.

Building a Resilient Support System

Since humans are social beings, having healthy connections is frequently associated with our capacity to overcome hardship.

Strong social ties increase a person's likelihood of overcoming adversity, according to studies.

Being around encouraging people helps us feel like we belong and serves as a reminder that we are not facing our challenges alone.

What if the voice in your brain has just been telling lies? What if your uncertainties, anxieties, and hesitancies are simply reverberations of past insecurities attempting to prevent you from moving forward? Resilience and confidence are not magical qualities that are only possessed by a select few. They are developed daily by the decisions we make and the stories we choose to believe.

Developing confidence is about learning to act despite fear, not about getting rid of it. It's about recognizing that you are more competent than you have been taught to believe. Moreover, it's about accepting suffering as it leads to progress.

Are you prepared to change your story? That is the true question. Because you have always held the pen.

CHAPTER 8
The Stories We Tell Ourselves

The Reality We Construct

The human mind does not merely see reality, but constructs stories as well. We construct a narrative around each incident, emotion, and decision we make in an attempt to understand our world. Our actions, ideas, and personas are all modelled after these stories. The problem is that most of these stories are influenced by perception, not reality. Plus, as we know, anxiety, insecurity, and experience often colour our perception.

To bring order out of chaos, our brain constructs stories that support our pre-existing ideas, whether they are beneficial to us or not. To match the narrative we've unknowingly selected, selects memories, eliminates irrelevant information, and distorts reality. This explains why two people may experience identical circumstances and emerge with quite different views. While the first sees a lesson, the second sees failure. One observes rejection, while the other observes rerouting. The distinction between progress and stagnation lies in the narrative we tell ourselves.

The Lies We Mistake for Truth

- "I'm not good enough." Possibly the most prevalent self-imposed falsehood is this one. Our brain compiles all of our shortcomings, criticisms, and failures and weaves them into a story of inadequacy. It persuades us that we are essentially defective, incapable of happiness, and unworthy of achievement. The irony is that this narrative is based on selective memories, excluding all successes and strong points.

- "This is just who I am." We become victims of self-fulfilling prophecies when we think that our habits, anxieties, and personalities are set in stone. Because change is unpredictable and uncertainty feels scary, the brain opposes change and wants continuity. Thus, it provides us with a narrative that maintains our current state of safety, predictability, and stagnation.
- "I have no choice." One of the most harmful stories our minds create is the one about powerlessness. It makes us believe that we are helpless to alter our circumstances and that we are at the mercy of our circumstances. However, the tale itself is frequently the only thing preventing us from moving on.

How Our Brain Twists the Past

Memory is an editing tool, not a recording device. Our brains rewrite the past to fit our pre-existing ideas, despite our assumption that our memories of events are true. Because of this, a person with low self-esteem may recall embarrassing or rejected experiences far more clearly than successful ones. This is the reason nostalgia may ensnare us in regret or longing, by making the past seem better than it was. The brain is more concerned with consistency than it is with the truth. It will emphasize memories that confirm your perception that you are worthless. If you think you are unlucky, it will ensure that you only remember the instances in which things didn't work out.

The Psychological Angle

Psychologists refer to this phenomenon as memory distortion, whereby our thoughts modify the past based on our present emotional state. According to research in cognitive psychology, we make little adjustments to memories each time we recall them. This suggests that our memories are dynamic and evolve. When we question ourselves, our past seems to be a series of failures. When we're upset, we may only remember the good aspects of a past relationship, which might make us feel as though we have lost something perfect when, in reality, we have lost something far more ideal.

The Scientific Angle

According to neuroscientific theory, the hippocampus, which is important for memory formation, does not store information like a hard drive. It uses incomplete knowledge to reconstruct events, adding biases and assumptions to fill in the blanks. Recalling a memory reinforces the brain connections associated with that version of the event, according to neurobiological studies. This means that the more we think about something skewedly, the more "real" it seems to us. This is the reason why humans can form false memories, which are completely made-up memories that seem as real as actual ones.

The Philosophical Angle

There have been arguments over how malleable reality is about what the human mind perceives it to be for centuries. Existentialists offer that rather than being concrete facts, our past is an interpretation that we create for ourselves so that we may attribute meaning to it. Friedrich Nietzsche is quoted as saying, "There are no facts, only interpretations." This is to say that our history is always changing and evolving, a never-ending story based on our current state of mind. We become trapped in a cycle of constant self-doubt and regret when we allow negative stories to define who we are and what we do in the future.

The Narratives That Keep Us Stuck

- The victim story: The idea that life is happening to us instead of for us, is known as the victim story. It deprives us of accountability and traps us in never-ending cycles of anger and blame. We give up control over our own lives when we think we are powerless. This story, which frequently draws from previous mistakes or betrayals, persuades us that the world is unjust. The truth is that although we have no control over everything that occurs to us, we do have some influence over how we react to it. The first step to regaining control of our lives is to abandon the victim narrative.
- The perfectionist: A tale that convinces us that unless something is flawless, it is worthless. This leads to procrastination, exhaustion, and chronic dissatisfaction. The brain feeds us this lie because it

is afraid of failing. "Don't do it at all if you don't do it perfectly," it says. This results in lost chances, crippling uncertainty, and pressure from the inside that makes even small tasks seem impossible. Accepting flaws is crucial for progress and mental well-being.

- Someday chant: We deceive ourselves that contentment, prosperity, or pleasure will always come later. "I'll be happy when..." delays life indefinitely, making it one of the most hazardous mental traps. The brain, which is constantly looking for solace, adores the notion that change may be postponed. It informs us that the appropriate moment will arrive later and that we are not yet ready. However, later never materializes. In actuality, life is occurring right now, and we miss the present when we wait for a hypothetically ideal time.
- The scarcity loop: It is the conviction that there is never enough time, money, love, or success for everyone. This kind of thinking encourages anxiety, rivalry, and comparison. The dread of missing out is a result of the brain's survival-wired continual threat-scanning. It persuades us to hold onto what we have, regardless of how harmful or unsatisfying it may be. Changing our perspective from one of scarcity to one of abundance enables us to recognize opportunities rather than constraints.

Recognizing Limiting Beliefs and Rewriting Our Personal Story Because our imaginations are powerful storytellers, we can make up tales about who we are, what we deserve, and what we can accomplish. What happens, therefore, is that these stories become prisons that trap us in cycles of fear, uncertainty, and self-defeating behaviour. Limiting beliefs are unconscious assumptions about our worth, aptitude, and place in the world that can quietly govern our lives without our awareness.

The Invisible Chains of Limiting Beliefs

This phenomenon, which psychologists refer to as the self-fulfilling prophecy, occurs when we unintentionally take actions that reinforce our beliefs. You could turn away from facing difficulties if you think you're doomed to fail, guaranteeing defeat before you even begin. You might settle for relationships that support your notion that you are unlovable. The brain holds onto these false certainties, persuading us that stepping outside of them is harmful, to shield us from suffering.

Questioning the Narrative: The First Step to Change

The first action to re-telling your tale is to question it. Question yourself: Where did this belief originate? Is it based on the truth, or merely an old hurt disguised as wisdom? A lot of our limiting beliefs are inherited—ones that have been passed down by family members who projected their fears onto us, teachers who doubted us, or failures from the past that were merely part of the growing process, not evidence of deficiency.

A useful exercise is evidence collection—write down a limiting belief and then come up with examples that disprove it. If you think you're "bad at relationships," remember times when you were kind, loyal, or empathetic. If you think you're "not good enough," think about past successes, no matter how minor. The brain is programmed to focus on bad experiences (a process known as negativity bias), so actively looking for counter-evidence serves to break the false narrative.

The Power of Rewriting Your Story

When we see the distorted stories that build our world, we can also rewrite them. This isn't about avoiding previous setbacks or denying that suffering exists—it's about changing how we look at things. Rather than labelling defeat as evidence of lack, view it as a learning curve. Rather than determining yourself by previous failures, re-determine yourself as someone who learns, adapts, and continues.

One of the methods employed in cognitive-behavioural therapy (CBT) is, cognitive restructuring, wherein negative thoughts are confronted and replaced with healthier, more empowering ones. If your inner voice tells you, "I'm not talented enough," change it to: "I'm constantly learning and improving." If you tell yourself, "I always mess up," change it to: "Mistakes are part of growth, and I get better every time."

Words are powerful. The words you speak to yourself will create your outside world. Begin to talk to yourself the same way you would to a friend—positively, lovingly, and kindly.

Living Beyond the Limits of the Mind

Eliminating limiting beliefs requires daily dedication to putting self-belief above self-doubt; it is not a quick fix. It calls for patience, deliberate work, and even painful progress. However, the benefits are enormous. Increased self-assurance, improved judgment, improved relationships, and the capacity to follow goals without putting obstacles in the way of oneself.

Ask yourself if the tale your brain tells you about who you are is true or if it's just a screenplay you've been reading for too long. If the latter is true, it's time to take up the pen and write a new narrative that liberates, inspires, and empowers you.

How to Create a Mindset That Empowers Rather Than Restricts

Our reality is powerfully constructed by our brain. It creates the prism through which we view the world, impacting our choices, self-assurance, and capacity for development. But far too frequently, we unintentionally erect barriers that impede our growth rather than fostering a mental environment that supports advancement. Changing our perspective from one that limits us to one that empowers us is the key to opening the door to a life of increased fulfilment and self-belief.

The Power of Perception: Choosing Expansion Over Limitation Perception colors everything that occurs in life. Even when two individuals have the same experience, their inner stories might lead them to see it very differently. The problem is that we often default to uncertainty, caution, and hesitancy because our minds are hardwired to shield instead of expanding our views. We must do something to actively challenge our perspectives.

What if we viewed challenges as training areas instead of obstacles? What if failure were viewed as proof of courage instead of a failure indicator? We construct our point of view to be one that propels us forward instead of leaving us stagnant in fear by making a conscious effort to alter the way we view things.

Reframing Fear: The Mindset Shift That Changes Everything Fear is one of the primary things that keeps limiting our thought patterns. It tells stories of failure, rejection, and humiliation that have little basis in reality. Fear is not necessarily a negative thing, however, and the problem is the way we respond to it.

Fear needs to be reframed as a challenge rather than a danger to create an empowered mindset. Fear is a sign of development, a chance to step beyond our comfort zones and realize our full potential. All successful people experience fear, but what sets them apart is that they choose to keep going despite it. We give ourselves the capacity to grow indefinitely when we accept fear as a compass rather than a barrier.

The Language of Self-Talk: Rewriting Your Mental Dialogue How we talk to ourselves makes a difference. Our internal monologue is the most constant voice we'll ever hear, and it can energize or deplete us. Most of us unconsciously affirm our limitations by habitually repeating words like:

"I'm not good enough."

"I'm too old to begin anew."

"I'll never be as successful as they are."

A more empowering attitude starts with a shift in language. Rather than statements affirming self-doubt, use instead:

"I am still learning, and every step forward is progress."

"I can grow at any point in life."

"My path is mine alone, and comparison does not benefit me."

It may seem awkward at first, but as with any habit, repeated exposure to positive affirmations reprograms the brain over time. Talk to yourself the way you would to a good friend—supportive, compassionate, and full of faith.

The Role of Action: Mindset is Built Through Movement

Mindset is not a mental practice—it is reinforced through action. We can't think our way to confidence; we have to demonstrate to ourselves that we are capable through experience. The solution is to make small, purposeful steps toward growth.

If you have trouble with self-doubt, tackle a small challenge that increases confidence—such as speaking up in a meeting or attempting something new outside of your comfort zone.

If you are afraid of failure, make a goal where failure is a possibility but growth is inevitable—such as learning something new or going for an opportunity even if you don't feel qualified.

If you struggle with negative self-talk, list down all self-critical thoughts and turn them into a positive statement.

Through action, you give undeniable proof to your brain that you are capable, flexible, and resilient.

Breaking Free: The Path to Mental Liberation

Developing an attitude that energizes instead of limits is not blind optimism or denial of fact. It's about taking charge of the narrative we create in our heads and deciding to look for possibilities where we had previously seen confines.

Imagine your life as it would be if you truly had faith in yourself. If failures weren't failures, they were stepping stones. If ambiguity wasn't a dead end, it was an open field. This shift in perspective is the cornerstone of a life of development, fulfilment, and purpose; it is not a sentimental endeavour.

For far too long, your brain has been your worst adversary. However, it may also be your greatest friend if you want it to be. So, are you prepared to turn around your story?

CHAPTER 9
The Comparison Rat Race

Comparison is ingrained in our minds and that is how we interpret the environment. However, this inclination may lead to feelings of inadequacy, anger, and even melancholy if it becomes a habit of constantly comparing oneself to others. Comparing is a deeply rooted survival strategy, not merely an old habit. But in today's culture, it does more harm than good.

How the Brain Tricks Us into Feeling Inferior

The mind is adept at tricking us into thinking that we're constantly lagging. It continuously looks for distinctions, and stresses the things that others possess that we do not. Our predecessors had to determine their position within a group to guarantee access to resources and safety, therefore this is an old survival habit. Today, though, this tendency shows itself as needless self-doubt. We presume someone has it all figured out when they succeed in an area where we fail. The brain readily overlooks difficulties, leading us to believe that we are fundamentally deficient.

The negative bias of our brains amplifies this propensity. Our attention is naturally drawn to imagined dangers, and in the modern environment, these dangers frequently manifest as personal failings. We wind up downplaying our strengths and exaggerating our shortcomings. This skewed view of oneself eventually results in diminished self-worth and a feeling of always falling behind.

The Brain's Obsession with Hierarchy

Another significant force in play is the brain's preference for ranking. From the beginning of human existence, social pecking orders have been central to survival. Understanding where one ranked in the pecking order determined one's access to resources and social standing. Although this impulse once served a useful purpose, it now appears as an unhealthy preoccupation with success, status, and outside approval.

We naturally position ourselves on a ladder in our mind, continually measuring whether we are higher or lower than others. The issue is that the ladder is always in flux—someone will always be doing better, accomplishing more, or seem happier. The ongoing mental hierarchy produces a vicious cycle of dissatisfaction. The mind assures us that ascending the social ladder will satisfy us, but the moment we attain a superior rung, it lowers the standard, leaving us pursuing a fantasy.

The Illusion of a Level-Playing Field

The idea that everyone starts from the same place and that success is only dependent on effort is one of the biggest myths our brains perpetuate. This is not at all the case. Individuals have various conditions, opportunities, and privileges depending on their background. However, we often ignore these aspects when evaluating ourselves against others. Instead, we internalize our difficulties and assume that our flaws are solely our fault.

Because it disregards context, the comparison is frequently unjust. Comparing two competitors in a race without recognizing one began kilometres ahead is analogous to that. However, these differences are not taken into consideration by the brain. It only fills the void within its judgment after noticing it.

The Dangers of Social Media and Unrealistic Expectations

The brain is caught up in a never-ending cycle of comparison in a world where social media has become an integral part of our everyday lives, continuously evaluating our value against the carefully chosen highlights of others. Already predisposed to seek approval, the mind is now exposed to a fake world that is meant to take advantage of our flaws. What begins as harmless scrolling quickly turns into a destructive cycle of self-doubt, jealousy, and an unquenchable desire for acceptance. Even worse, the more we interact, the more we become engrossed in this delusion, without realizing that we are only pursuing a false impression that was produced by algorithms meant to keep us interested.

The Illusion of Perfection

- Selective Reality: Social media presents a filtered view of people's lives, highlighting only their most noteworthy moments, such as beautifully shot photographs, opulent vacations, professional peaks, and seemingly simple successes. However, the selective nature of these postings is not recognized by the brain. Instead, it views this data in its entirety, setting an impossible standard for success and satisfaction. The more of this material we consume, the more we feel that our own lives are inadequate. We begin measuring our achievement by the distorted yardstick of someone else's online presence instead of our growth.

- Fake Happiness: Individuals will stop at nothing to create the ideal online identity. To increase their perceived significance, some even purchase likes, views, and followers. What they don't understand is that they are lying to themselves as well as to others. Anxiety and a long-standing dread of being "exposed" as normal are fueled by this continual urge to preserve the appearance of accomplishment.

Dopamine and the Addiction to Approval

- The Chemical Hijack: Every like, comment, and share releases dopamine, a pleasure reward neurotransmitter. Social media has hijacked this system, which was originally meant to reinforce survival skills, to keep us addicted. We begin relying on others' validation, seeking it from people we don't see or know much about. High engagement is thrilling, but low engagement is a sharp drop in self-esteem. Our mental and emotional health is impacted by this dependence, and we begin to be more concerned with being seen rather than with true self-improvement.

- The Toll on the Body and Mind: Addiction to social media hurts both mental and physical health. Nonstop scrolling causes eye strain, poor posture, high stress levels, and sleep loss. This reliance on technology eventually leads to a sedentary lifestyle that compromises mental and physical fortitude. Social media creates false dopamine loops that cause us to retreat more and more from real-world events.

The Comparison Spiral

In contrast to interactions in real life, where flaws and challenges are evident, social media gives the impression of effortless perfection. When we compare our unfiltered reality to the highlights of other people's lives, we expose ourselves to disappointment. The brain does not comprehend that these images are carefully selected, often enhanced by skilled editing and witty storytelling. Instead, it gives us the impression that we are falling behind, less prosperous, less desirable, and ultimately less valuable. This mindset creates anxiety and low self-esteem and fosters an unhealthy obsession with living up to false standards.

The Brain's Obsession with Hierarchy

- The Necessity for Social Rank: We are built to evaluate our position about others. Knowing one's position within the tribe meant having access to resources and protection, which was essential for survival in prehistoric times. But in the contemporary world, this primival impulse shows up in dangerous ways, especially on social media.

- Status anxiety: The brain continuously assesses our social position, and worry is triggered when we believe we are lower on the hierarchy. This is known as status anxiety. The brain mistakenly associates riches, beauty, and fame with security and happiness. This makes us prone to pursuing status symbols.

Detachment from Reality and the Metaverse Deception

- Losing Touch with the Real World: Social media has evolved into another universe where maintaining friendships is no longer the goal. Many people have lost touch with their actual lives as a result of the emergence of influencers, digital personalities, and even virtual realms like the metaverse. People engage in shallow and frequently fraudulent online contacts rather than developing deep, in-person relationships.
- The Escapism Loop: The mind turns to social media as an escape when reality seems threatening. People's real lives get less developed the more they interact with their virtual ones. People feel more at ease in virtual reality than in real life, and the metaverse's vision of a completely digital world only widens this divide.

Shifting from Comparison to Self-Improvement

Shifting our attention from outward validation to internal progress is the right key to breaking away from the cycle of comparison, and not ignoring the world around us. The secret is to reinterpret such observations in a way that promotes personal growth rather than self-doubt, instead of ceasing to recognize the distinctions between ourselves and other people. We may use comparison as a tool for learning, self-improvement, and inspiration rather than as a gauge of inferiority.

1. The Power of Self-Awareness

Being conscious is the first step in avoiding the comparison trap. We frequently make unconscious comparisons to ourselves when we browse social media or look at our friends, instantly ranking ourselves. We need to stop and examine our ideas to recover control:

Is this comparison beneficial or detrimental to me?

Am I holding myself to a reasonable and equitable standard?

Does this make me feel less valuable or does it motivate me to develop?

We should refocus our attention on what truly matters—our path—by being aware of when and why we compare.

2. Redefining Success on Your Terms

Society, social media, and cultural standards enforce a rigid definition of success that includes riches, celebrity, beauty, and status. These external markers, however, are arbitrary and flexible. Self-respect, fulfillment, and purpose are key components of true success, which is very personalized. Instead of going after what seems good, think about this:

What does success mean to me?

What kind of life do I want to build?

Is my desire or outside pressure driving me to pursue a goal? Redefining success to fall within your criteria reduces the need for comparison since you are now competing in your race rather than someone else's.

3. Focus on Progress, Not Perfection

Our brains are wired to pursue perfection, even when it is an illusion. Concentrate on your development and not an idealized vision of the person you should be:

Celebrate little triumphs. Development happens in little, incremental steps.

Monitor your journeys. Maintain a journal, take note of your progress, and reflect on your achievements.

Emphasize effort more than the outcome. There are times when the process is more crucial than the outcome.

Each step taken forward is a success if you value progression above perfection, so comparisons are futile.

4. Practicing Gratitude to Shift Perspective

The attitude of scarcity, which holds that our accomplishment is less significant than others, is conducive to comparison. By turning our attention from what we lack to what we have, and by inculcating a sense of gratitude we can combat this. Rather than letting someone else's life make you feel inadequate, tell yourself:

What do I already have for which I am thankful?

In what ways have I changed since a year ago?

What distinguishing characteristics define who I am?

Being grateful is a mental reset. By rewiring the brain to emphasize an abundance, rather than a shortage, it transforms self-improvement from a punishment into an opportunity.

5. Detoxing from the Triggers of Comparison

If social media, specific people, or specific environments make you feel inadequate, it might be time for a detox. Maintaining your mental space is as important as maintaining your physical health.

Consider:

Unfollowing accounts that make you feel smaller. Reducing mindless scrolling by limiting screen usage. Surrounding yourself with people who make you feel better rather than worse.

Engaging in rewarding and pleasurable activities in the actual world. The goal of removing comparison triggers is to create a more pleasant environment where self-improvement may flourish without constant self-criticism, and avoiding reality.

6. Learning from Others Instead of Competing

Not everything that can be compared is negative. By design, healthy comparison is distinguished from destructive comparison. Instead of viewing others' successes as evidence of your failure, view them as:

Inspirational source: What can I learn from their experience?

Advice: What techniques or strategies helped them succeed?

Cooperation: How do I reach out to others who agree with me so that we can grow together?

Comparison can become an incentive for self-improvement when used as a didactic device and not as an instrument of self-punishment.

Conclusion: Your Only Competition is You

The fundamental conflict here is not with others, but with ourselves. A survival strategy that no longer works for us in the modern world is the brain's fixation with comparison. It is within our power to change the story.

What if we concentrated on where we are today in comparison to where we were yesterday rather than where we stand in comparison to others? What if developing our best selves, rather than becoming the greatest, was the key to success? What if we worked together, gained knowledge, and developed as a team rather than competing with the outside world?

The person you were yesterday is the only one you need to improve upon. The others? Not important. Give it up and concentrate on crafting your narrative.

CHAPTER 10
The Power of Reprogramming

How to Take Control of Our Thoughts and Behaviors

Though most of us live our lives without realizing how deeply rooted mental patterns influence our emotions, decisions, and behaviors, ideas do create our world. Although we prefer to think we are in charge, the fact is that our brains function automatically, carrying out the same patterns of thinking and behavior that were ingrained in us years ago. The good news? We can rewire our brains.

Understanding the secret scripts operating in our subconscious and consciously rewriting them is the goal of reprogramming, not making ourselves "think positively" or repressing bad feelings. It involves overcoming limiting, outmoded thought habits and forming empowering new ones. How can we accomplish it? Let's get started with regaining control.

The Brain as a Supercomputer: Running Old Software

Imagine your brain as a powerful computer. Its software was installed in early life—programmed by experience, conditioning, and personal belief. Fossilized software clogs an engine like that. Stale thinking gets stuck in unproductive loops. Mental software needs updating to change.

- Neural Pathways and Habit Loops: All behavior and thinking lead to neural pathways in the brain becoming stronger. The more we practice a behavior or a way of thinking, the more it is strengthened—similar to a frequently traveled trail in the woods. That is why unhelpful habits and negative thinking patterns seem automatic.
- The Power of Neuroplasticity: Fortunately, the brain can change. Neuroplasticity, the brain's capacity to rewire, enables us to unlearn old habits and learn new ones. But it takes effort, persistence, and time.

The Role of Self-Awareness: Identifying the Hidden Programs

We must become conscious of our ideas before we can alter them. The majority of our brain programming functions subconsciously, affecting us without our knowledge. The first step in altering these subconscious behaviors is in acknowledging them.

Take Note of Your Thoughts:

Keep an eye out for negative ideas that keep cropping up. When you make a mistake, what do you tell yourself? When you encounter a difficulty, how do you proceed? When do you evaluate yourself against others?

Disprove Automatic Beliefs:

A lot of the assumptions we make about ourselves are based on conditioning from society or prior experiences rather than on reality. Is this belief helping me, you ask? Is it true at all?

Develop Mindfulness:

Being aware of our inner monologue enables us to break harmful thought patterns and make room for fresh, purposeful ideas.

Reprogramming the Mind: Practical Strategies

We may start substituting restricting ideas with powerful ones as soon as we recognize them. Here's how:

Cognitive Reframing: Reframe negative ideas in a way that strengthens you rather than taking them at face value. For instance, substitute, "I always fail," with "Every failure is an opportunity to learn and grow."

Resonant Affirmations: Positive affirmations must feel genuine to encourage new brain connections. Say "I am learning to become more confident every day" rather than "I am confident" when you don't believe it.

Visualization: The brain is incapable of telling the difference between imagined and real events. The mind can be trained to anticipate success and favorable results by visualizing them.

Behavioral Shifts: Action and thought retraining are most effective when combined. Start by performing little, disciplined acts every day if you wish to think of yourself as disciplined. The brain picks up knowledge through experience.

Breaking Free from Emotional Conditioning

Most of our programming in the unconscious is rooted in fear— primarily fear. Programming in fear causes us to play small, we are afraid to rock the boat, and question our abilities. To gain control of our thoughts, we need to break ourselves from this emotional conditioning.

Understanding Fear Responses: If you are anxious or afraid, then it is probably an old emotional program. Rather than responding from impulse, stop and ask yourself if the fear is rational or if it is only an old script.

Exposure Therapy: Slow exposure is the strongest method to rewire fear-based thinking. The more we slowly expose ourselves to our fears in tiny, manageable doses, the more our brains get the message that they're not as scary as we think.

Emotional Regulation Techniques: Emotional regulation techniques such as breathing, meditation, and journaling can be used to cope with emotions and to calm automatic old fear-based responses from occurring.

The Science Behind Neuroplasticity and Habit Change

Our brains are dynamic, flexible, and continuously rewiring themselves in response to our experiences, ideas, and actions; they are not static, unalterable machines. All learning and the development of habits are based on this capacity of our brains, which is called neuroplasticity. It implies that with deliberate effort and repetition, any habit or belief— no matter how deeply embedded—can be altered.

Understanding Neuroplasticity: The Brain's Ability to Rewire Itself

Neuroplasticity is the ability of the brain to reorganize itself by forming new neural connections throughout life. Every time we think, practice a skill, or do a behavior, our brain strengthens the neural pathways for that action. The more we do it, the more powerful the pathway becomes—similar to digging a deeper rut in a dirt road with repeated travel.

- Synaptic Pruning: Our brain eliminates redundant neural connections and enhances frequently used ones. That's why repetitive acts and thoughts come naturally, while neglected skills slowly break down.
- Hebbian Learning: Often referred to as "neurons that fire together, wire together," this process explains how habitual pairings between actions and ideas make brain connections stronger.
- Neurogenesis: In contrast to the past, the brain can generate new neurons even in adulthood, especially in regions linked with learning and memory, such as the hippocampus.

Breaking Old Habits: Why Change Feels Difficult

If neuroplasticity means change, then why are so many people unable to change bad habits? The answer lies in the way our brains prioritize efficiency. Habits form because the brain is conserving energy. Once an act is performed a sufficient number of times, it moves from thinking to automaticity—so the brain can focus on something else.

But to break a habit is to disrupt those automatic associations and form new ones, and that feels hard and unnatural at first. Here's why:

The Habit Loop: Habits are a cycle of cue, routine, and reward, neuroscientist, Charles Duhigg describes. To change a habit, we must identify and alter one of these elements.

Dopamine and Reward Systems: We release dopamine in our brain when we perform a rewarding action, reinforcing the action. Unhealthy habits like junk food, laziness, or excessive social media use, hijack this system, so they're difficult to abandon.

Resistance to Change: Basal ganglia in our brain hold habits in place, making them automatic. It takes effort again and again to rewire these circuits before the new habit sets in and replaces the old one.

The Process of Habit Change: Rewiring the Brain Step by Step

To reprogram our brains and behaviors effectively, we need to work at breaking habits step by step. Here's how:

1. Identify Triggers and Patterns: Note what triggers the habit you want to change. Is it stress, boredom, or some setting?

2. Replace Rather Than Erase: Don't just eliminate an unwanted habit. Replace it with a new, better habit that satisfies the same craving. For example, replace mindless scrolling with reading or stretching.

3. Utilize Implementation Intentions: Develop specific cues and actions, such as "When I feel stressed, I will take five deep breaths instead of reaching for my phone."

4. Make It Easy: Ensure good habits are easy to achieve and bad ones hard to execute. To exercise, set aside your exercise attire the evening before. To curtail social media, logout from the platforms or turn off the notifications.

5. Reinforce with Rewards: The brain responds well to reward. Reward little triumphs in order to sustain levels of motivation and reinforce new conduct.

6. Embracing Repetition and Patience: The mind needs to be repeatedly exposed to new behavior to anchor them. Habit formation takes, on average, 66 days, according to research—but speed is no match for consistency.

Emotional and Cognitive Strategies for Reprogramming

Long-lasting transformation requires not just behavioral tactics but also mental and emotional adjustments:

- Cognitive Reframing: Consciously substitute powerful ideas for self-defeating thoughts.
- Mindfulness and meditation strengthen the prefrontal cortex and can help us overcome impulsive behavior and make more deliberate decisions.
- Journaling and Self-Reflection: Recording our progress in writing facilitates tracking and strategy adjustment while also reinforcing learning.

Steps to Rewire the Brain for Long-Term Achievement

1. Brain-overhaul isn't just about breaking negative habits—it's about creating long-term success through the right behaviors and mindset. These are the necessary steps:
2. Make a Commitment to Growth: Transformation requires an inner commitment. Realize that mind-reprogramming is a lifetime process.
3. Be Surrounded by Positive Influences: Who and what you surround yourself with, shapes your mind. Make the world around you positive and supportive.
4. Have a Learning Mindset: Instead of fearing failure, view every failure as a chance to learn and grow. Learning is the way to make neural connections stronger.
5. Use Small, Consistent Actions: Consistent small action leads to long-term change, but not large erratic action.
6. Celebrate Progress: Reward and acknowledge yourself for every improvement, no matter how small. Reinforcement strengthens neural pathways.
7. Keep Adapting: Your habits and your mind will evolve in the long term. Be adaptable and change your approach as needed.

The Champion Within You

If anything motivates you from this, let it be this: you are not broken, you are not weak, and you are not stuck. Your brain might have told you that you're a captive of your past, your fears, and your doubts—but you are stronger than you know.

There is a champion inside every one of us—a potential and waiting-to-be-seen toughness. It could have been hidden deep inside for many years, under the weight of unsuccessful attempts, under the burden of the world's expectations. It is there, though. It always was.

Remember, each and every time you believed you were going to make it, you did. Each time you fell, miraculously, through the pain, you got up once more. Each time you doubted yourself, something deep within you said, keep going. That voice? That flame? That's your champion. And now it's time to bring it to life.

Your mind will protest. It will struggle to cage you in safe habits, because the unknown is frightening. But the real horror is to remain the same. Waking up years from now, knowing you never gave yourself a chance to live, to be courageous, to pursue what ignited your flame.

You don't need to be perfect. You don't need to be fearless. You just need to begin. One shift, one step, one choice at a time. Because here's the thing: you are already enough. The champion within you isn't something you need to become—it's something you need to recall.

And when you finally do glimpse it, when you finally shed the shackles your mind has placed upon you, you will see: you were never your enemy. You were always your greatest strength.

Now go. Take back control. The world is waiting for the real you.